Banking Language

A SURVIVAL VOCABULARY

Jim Richey

Reading Specialist

Illustrated by Ed Tadiello

GLOBE FEARON

Pearson Learning Group

Janus Survival Vocabulary Books
Banking Language
Clothing Language
Credit Language
Driver's License Language
Drugstore Language
Entertainment Language
Job Application Language
Medical Language
Restaurant Language
Supermarket Language

ISBN 0-8359-1527-1
Printed in the United States of America
8 9 10   07 06

1-800-321-3106
www.pearsonlearning.com

Contents

Introduction

I have a cousin who used to hide her money in her house. One day, someone broke into her house and stole her money. My cousin lost every cent she had!

I asked her why she hadn't kept her money in the bank. My cousin told me she was afraid to go into a bank. Why? *Because she couldn't read the words banks used.*

So, I decided to teach her some useful banking (BANK ing)* words. I taught her words that are on bank signs, forms, and notices. And words that bank people use.

My cousin learned the words. And now, she keeps her money safe, in a bank. And she uses the bank for other things, too, such as getting a loan or cashing checks.

You can learn the banking words I taught my cousin. They are in this book. They helped her learn how to use a bank. They can help you, too.

*You will see a respelling like this after each new word in this book. To learn how to use the respellings, see page 48.

Unit One

Banking Hours Different banks are open at different hours. So, banks post signs to tell people when they are open. Between what hours is the bank above open?

_____

On what two days is the bank closed?

_____

_____

Pretest

- ☐ check
- ☐ bills
- ☐ coins
- ☐ slip
- ☐ funds
- ☐ fixed
- ☐ charge
- ☐ cash
- ☐ joint
- ☐ vault
- ☐ total
- ☐ forward
- ☐ payment
- ☐ record
- ☐ less cash

Fill in this slip to put money in the bank.

Words and Meanings

Say the banking word out loud and read its meaning. Read the sentence that follows. Then find and circle the banking word in the sentence. The first is done for you.

Check (CHEK): *a paper that orders a bank to give money to someone.*

He gave me a (check) for $10.

Bills (BILZ): *paper money.*

She had two $5 bills.

Coins (KOINZ): *money made of metal.*

Dimes, nickels, and pennies are coins.

Slip (SLIP): *a paper form used by banks.*

Fill in this slip to put money in the bank.

Funds (FUHNDZ): *money that can be used.*

They don't have the funds to pay their bills.

Same Words

Check the word in each row that is the same as the first word in the row. Go as fast as you can. Time yourself. The first one is done for you.

Coins	Corns	Cones	Coins ✓
Funds	Funds	Fun	Finds
Check	Chick	Check	Click
Bills	Bells	Bulls	Bills
Slip	Slop	Slip	Slap

No. Correct _____

Time _____

Missing Vowels

To finish these words, fill in the missing vowels. Write the complete words on the blank lines. The first is done for you.

fnds _____ *funds* _____

chck _____

cns _____

slp _____

blls _____

Scrambled Letters

The letters in each of the words are mixed up. Write the letters so they spell the words from the list at the top of page 7. The first one is done for you.

slibl _____ *bills* _____

ckceh _____

sonic _____

snufd _____

plis _____

Pick a Word

Underline the word that belongs in the space. Then write the word in the space. The first one is done for you.

He had a roll of one-dollar _____ *bills* _____ .

    bells   wills   <u>bills</u>

Dimes are _____ .

    dollars   coins   bills

They had the _____ to buy a house.

    friends   fans   funds

She wrote a _____ for $25.

    check   chick   funds

Did you forget to fill out the bank _____ ?

    coins   bills   slip

I'll pay for this with cash.

Words and Meanings

Say the banking word out loud and read its meaning. Read the sentence that follows. Then find and circle the banking word in the sentence.

Fixed (FIXT): *not changing.*

He pays a fixed fee every month to park his car.

Charge (CHAHRJ): *fee paid for something.*

There is a charge for this bank plan.

Cash (KASH): *bills and coins.*

I'll pay for this with cash.

Joint (JOINT): *belonging to two or more people.*

They have a joint checking plan at the bank.

Vault (VAWLT): *strong place to keep things safe.*

The bank keeps its money in a vault.

Same Words

Check the word in each row that is the same as the first word in the row. Go as fast as you can. Time yourself.

Vault	Value	Vault	Fault
Fixed	Fired	Filled	Fixed
Cash	Catch	Cost	Cash
Joint	Joint	Join	Jaunt
Charge	Change	Charge	Chart

No. Correct _____

Time _____

Letter Squares

The letters in each square spell a word from the list at the top of page 9. Write the word below the square. The first one is done for you.

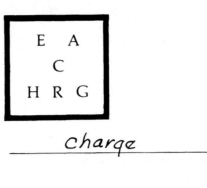

charge

Missing Ink

Complete the words by adding a curve or a straight line to each letter. Then write the words on the blank lines. The first one is done for you.

CASH _____ *cash* _____

VAULT _____

JOINT _____

FIXED _____

CHARGE _____

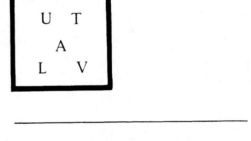

_____

Pick a Word

Underline the word that belongs in the space. Then write the word in the space.

A _____ is a safe place to keep money.
    vault   fault   fee

She paid for the food with _____ .
    joint   slip   cash

Is there a _____ for this bank plan?
    funds   charge   change

He and his wife have a _____ checking plan.
    point   blank   joint

Every month he pays a _____ fee of $10.
    fixed   fast   safety

**Do you keep a record
of the checks you write?**

Words and Meanings

Say the banking word out loud and read its meaning. Read the sentence that follows. Then find and circle the banking word in the sentence.

Total (TOHT uhl): *everything added up.*

The total of her cash and checks is $400.

Forward (FAWR werd): *move to another place.*

Forward the total of your checks to the other side of the bank slip.

Payment (PAY muhnt): *money paid for something.*

They make a house payment each month.

Record (REK erd): *written facts about something or someone.*

Do you keep a record of the checks you write?

Less Cash (LES KASH): *cash given you when you put checks in your bank plan.*

On your bank slip, write how much cash you want where it says "Less Cash."

Same Words

Check the word in each row that is the same as the first word in the row. Go as fast as you can. Time yourself.

Less Cash	Less Wash	Let Crash	Less Cash
Forward	Forworn	Forward	Fortune
Total	Total	Hotel	Toter
Record	Recount	Record	Reverse
Payment	Pavement	Paycheck	Payment

No. Correct _____

Time _____

Word Wheel

Begin at Start. Find the first word. Put a line between it and the next word. One word follows another. Write the words on the lines as you find them. The first one is done for you.

less cash _____

_____

_____

_____

_____

Start ▶ L E S S C A S H | T O T A L P A Y M E N T R E C O R D F O R W A R D

Scrambled Letters

The letters in each of the words are mixed up. Write the letters so they spell words from the list at the top of page 11.

decror _____

sels shac _____

tenmayp _____

lotat _____

rawford _____

Pick a Word

Underline the word that belongs in the space. Then write the word in the space.

His _____ funds added up to $100.

      vault   total   toter

She asked for $20 _____ .

    last cost   let catch   less cash

They made a _____ for their new car.

    payment   slip   cash

The bank kept a _____ of what she paid.

    pocket   vault   record

_____ the total to the next page.

    Forworn   Forget   Forward

Review

The 15 words and phrases listed below are hidden in the puzzle. They are all printed in a straight line. But they may read across, up, down, backwards, or on a slant. Some words overlap. Circle the words and phrases as you find them. Then cross them off the list. One is done for you.

COINS   JOINT
FUNDS   VAULT
CHECK   TOTAL
BILLS   FORWARD
SLIP   PAYMENT
FIXED   RECORD
CHARGE   LESS CASH
CASH

```
D W D B F T X S T H S A C
R T Q U U H C B K O W R P
A P F J N X T O T A L O O
W P A U D M O E V L D R L
R T H Y S L A J Z E Y F V
O J E I M G D O M S M B A
F S O T D E R I S S C C U
C A L R X E N N T C H H L
S P R I E S I T D A E N T
L O F F P T H E R S C N E
L I T E D S T G A H K E R
I S O F B M E R C I A V Y
B R E C O R D J C O I N S
```

Test

Put a + by the sentence that is true. Put a ○ by the sentence that is not true.

_____ 1. Coins are bills.

_____ 2. A bank slip is a small loan.

_____ 3. A joint plan is used by one person.

_____ 4. Funds are money that can be used.

_____ 5. A cost that is fixed changes every month.

_____ 6. A vault keeps money safe.

_____ 7. The bank keeps a record of how much money you put in it.

_____ 8. *Less cash* means money that is put in a bank.

_____ 9. You add to get a total.

_____ 10. *Forward* means the same as *payment*.

Unit Two

New Accounts   When you want to open a bank plan, do this: Talk to the bank person who handles New Accounts. That person will start the plan for you. Why might people want to keep their money in a bank?

_____

_____

_____

Pretest

- ☐ account
- ☐ apply
- ☐ insured
- ☐ checking
- ☐ savings
- ☐ percent
- ☐ submit
- ☐ pending
- ☐ statement
- ☐ balance
- ☐ transfer
- ☐ checkbook
- ☐ passbook
- ☐ deduct
- ☐ received

I'd like to apply for a small loan.

Words and Meanings

Say the banking word out loud and read its meaning. Read the sentence that follows. Then find and circle the banking word in the sentence.

Account (uh KOWNT): *a bank plan.*

Did you open an account at that bank?

Apply (uh PLIGH): *ask for something.*

I'd like to apply for a small loan.

Insured (in SHOORD): *safe from losing money.*

Most bank accounts are insured.

Checking (CHEK ing): *bank plan that uses checks.*

You can buy things with checks when you have a checking account.

Savings (SAYV ingz): *bank plan for saving money.*

He put $10 into his savings account.

Same Words

Check the word in each row that is the same as the first word in the row. Go as fast as you can. Time yourself.

Insured	Income	Insured	In case
Checking	Chopping	Checkers	Checking
Apply	April	Appoint	Apply
Savings	Savings	Safety	Sayings
Account	Amount	Accept	Account

No. Correct _____

Time _____

Letter Squares

The letters in each square spell a word from the list at the top of page 15. Write the word below the square.

```
Y   P
  A
P   L
```

_____

Missing Vowels

To finish these words, fill in the missing vowels. Write the complete words on the blank lines.

chckng _____

ccnt _____

svngs _____

nsrd _____

pply _____

```
C   N   U
      A
O   T   C
```

_____

Pick a Word

Underline the word that belongs in the space. Then write the word in the space.

An _____ is a bank plan.
    vault   charge   account

Your money is usually safe in the bank because
    it is _____ .
    in case   insured   inside

You can write checks if you have a _____
    account.
    savings   less cash   checking

You can save money in a _____
    account.
    savings   charge   checking

Did you _____ for a bank account?
    forward   apply   record

```
S   V   G
  N   S
A       I
```

_____

```
E   C   N
  I   K
G   C   H
```

_____

```
D   R   U
  I   S
  N   E
```

_____

The letter says, "Please submit payment for your electric light bill."

Words and Meanings

Say the banking word out loud and read its meaning. Read the sentence that follows. Then find and circle the banking word in the sentence.

Percent (per SENT): *a part of a whole.*
   A dime is 10 percent of a dollar.
Submit (suhb MIT): *give; send.*
   The letter says, "Please submit payment for your electric light bill."
Pending (PEND ing): *waiting to happen.*
   The loan was still pending.
Statement (STAYT muhnt): *notice that shows a record of a bank account.*
   The bank sent a statement of my checking account.
Balance (BAL uhns): *how much money is left.*
   The balance in your checking account is $25.

Same Words

Check the word in each row that is the same as the first word in the row. Go as fast as you can. Time yourself.

Statement	Shipment	Payment	Statement
Submit	Remit	Submit	Supply
Balance	Bandage	Balloon	Balance
Percent	Decent	Percent	Permit
Pending	Pending	Bending	Pealing

No. Correct _____

Time _____

Word Wheel

Begin at Start. Find the first word. Put a line between it and the next word. One word follows another. Write the words on the lines as you find them.

_____

_____

_____

_____

_____

Missing Ink

Complete the words by adding a curve or a straight line to each letter. Then write the words on the blank lines.

STATEMENT _____

PERCENT _____

SUBMIT _____

BALANCE _____

PENDING _____

Pick a Word

Underline the word that belongs in the space. Then write the word in the space.

A dime is 10 _____ of a dollar.

    percent   balance   accounts

Something that is yet to happen is _____.

    issued   pending   forward

The bank mails me a _____ every month.

    vault   teller   statement

The _____ is how much money you have in your account.

    savings   payment   balance

Please _____ payment for this bill.

    joint   qualify   submit

They received a statement from the bank.

Words and Meanings

Say the banking word out loud and read its meaning. Read the sentence that follows. Then find and circle the banking word in the sentence.

Transfer (TRANS fer): *move from one place to another.*
We'll have to transfer our funds to another bank.

Checkbook (CHEK buk): *a book of blank checks.*
She took a check from her checkbook.

Passbook (PAS buk): *book that keeps a record of a savings account.*
The bank marks your passbook whenever you put in or take out money.

Deduct (di DUHKT): *take away.*
Deduct $20 from my checking account.

Received (ri SEEVD): *got.*
He received a statement from the bank.

Same Words

Check the word in each row that is the same as the first word in the row. Go as fast as you can. Time yourself.

Passbook	Checkbook	Password	Passbook
Received	Received	Receipt	Reversed
Deduct	Deduce	Debit	Deduct
Transfer	Trainer	Transfer	Tractor
Checkbook	Checking	Passbook	Checkbook

No. Correct _____

Time _____

Missing Vowels

To finish these words, fill in the missing vowels. Write the complete words on the blank lines.

rcvd _____

chckbk _____

trnsfr _____

ddct _____

pssbk _____

Scrambled Letters

The letters in each of the words are mixed up. Write the letters so they spell words from the list at the top of page 19.

tedcud _____

sopoksab _____

chokobeck _____

diecreev _____

fastnerr _____

Pick a Word

Underline the word that belongs in the space. Then write the word in the space.

A _____ is used with savings accounts.
   passbook   checkbook   workbook

She signed the slip for the cash she _____ .
   received   balance   percent

A _____ is used with checking accounts.
   savings   checkbook   passbook

You get $19 when you _____ $11 from $30.
   submit   add   deduct

You may _____ money from one account to another.
   vault   transfer   checking

Unit Two

Review

The 15 words from the list on page 14 fit into this puzzle. They go across and down. The sentences and number of spaces will help you. As you find the words, write them in the spaces in the sentences. One is done for you.

Across

2. You save money with a ___savings___ account.
5. You can _____ for a bank loan.
6. The bank sent a _____.
8. _____ means to take away.
9. An _____ is a bank plan.
10. A dime is ten _____ of a dollar.
12. She _____ a letter.
14. You can write checks when you have a _____ account.

Down

1. The _____ is what is left.
2. _____ means to send.
3. Bank money is usually _____.
4. You need a _____ for your savings account.
7. You may _____ funds to another bank.
11. A _____ has blank checks.
13. _____ means yet to happen.

(crossword grid with 2 Across filled in: SAVINGS)

Test

Answer the questions below. Write *yes* or *no* in front of each of them.

_____ 1. Are checkbooks used for savings?
_____ 2. Do you add when you deduct?
_____ 3. When something is pending, is it happening now?
_____ 4. Do you need a passbook for a checking account?
_____ 5. Is money insured at the bank?

_____ 6. Would a statement show the balance in your checking account?
_____ 7. Is a plan a percent of a dime?
_____ 8. Can you submit money to a bank?
_____ 9. Does *received* mean got?
_____ 10. Can you transfer funds to another bank?

Unit Three

Loan Information (in fuhr MAY shuhn)
People who need money for certain reasons can ask a bank for a loan. Banks offer many different kinds of loans. What kind of loan does the person above want?

_____

Pretest

- [ ] service
- [ ] endorse
- [ ] issued
- [ ] teller
- [ ] presence
- [ ] trustee
- [ ] beginning
- [ ] interest
- [ ] traveler
- [ ] cashier
- [ ] deposit
- [ ] penalty
- [ ] regular
- [ ] notify
- [ ] outstanding

**This bank offers a
different kind of service.**

Words and Meanings

Say the banking word out loud and read its meaning. Read the sentence that follows. Then find and circle the banking word in the sentence.

Service (SER vuhs): *work done for someone; a helpful act.*

This bank offers a different kind of service.

Endorse (in DORS): *sign your name on the back of a check.*

You must endorse a paycheck to cash it.

Issued (ISH ood): *given out.*

The new dollar coins were issued by the bank.

Teller (TEL er): *person who takes in and gives out money in banks.*

She gave her passbook to the teller.

Presence (PREZ uhns): *in front of.*

Endorse this check in the presence of the teller.

Same Words

Check the word in each row that is the same as the first word in the row. Go as fast as you can. Time yourself.

Teller	Taller	Tiller	Teller
Service	Service	Server	Submit
Presence	Presents	Presence	Percent
Endorse	Endures	Endue	Endorse
Issued	Tissue	Issued	Isolate

No. Correct _____

Time _____

Letter Squares

The letters in each square spell a word from the list at the top of page 23. Write the word below the square.

Missing Ink

Complete the words by adding a curve or a straight line to each letter. Then write the words on the blank lines.

TELLER _____

SERVICE _____

PRESENCE _____

ENDORSE _____

ISSUED _____

Pick a Word

Underline the word that belongs in the space. Then write the word in the space.

Some checking accounts have a _____ charge.

    apply   service   received

She was _____ a new passbook.

    issued   fixed   forward

Give your money to the _____ .

    charge   safety   teller

Sign this slip in the _____ of the teller.

    safety   register   presence

_____ your check when you cash it.

    Apply   Transfer   Endorse

S	O	E
	E	R
	N	D

_____

P		E	S
	N		C
	E	E	R

_____

R		C
	E	E
S	V	I

_____

I	U	E
	S	D	S

_____

E	R	L
	L	T	E

_____

Don't leave without your traveler's checks!

Words and Meanings

Say the banking word out loud and read its meaning. Read the sentence that follows. Then find and circle the banking word in the sentence.

Trustee (truhs TEE): *someone who takes care of someone else's money.*

This child must have a trustee for his account.

Beginning (bi GIN ing): *starting.*

Your account earns money beginning now.

Interest (IN truhst): *money paid to use money.*

The bank pays interest on your savings account.

Traveler (TRAV uh ler): *person who goes on a trip.*

Don't leave without your traveler's checks!

Cashier (ka SHEAR): *a bank officer.*

The bank may give you a cashier's check.

Same Words

Check the word in each row that is the same as the first word in the row. Go as fast as you can. Time yourself.

Cashier	Cashier	Cashes	Cashew
Beginning	Balance	Behaving	Beginning
Interest	Issued	Interest	Payment
Trustee	Trusting	Trainee	Trustee
Traveler	Transfer	Traveler	Transact

No. Correct _____

Time _____

Word Wheel

Begin at Start. Find the first word. Put a line between it and the next word. One word follows another. Write the words on the lines as you find them.

_____

_____

_____

_____

_____

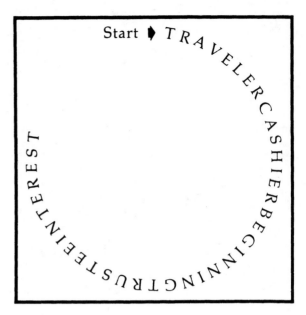

Scrambled Letters

The letters in each of the words are mixed up. Write the letters so they spell words from the list at the top of page 25.

eevlarrt _____

nibgengin _____

streetin _____

shacrie _____

ersteut _____

Pick a Word

Underline the word that belongs in the space. Then write the word in the space.

People use _____ 's checks on trips.

    traveler   joint   pending

His account is _____ to earn money.

    transfer   beginning   currency

She is the _____ for her son's account.

    charge   safety   trustee

Banks pay _____ on saving accounts.

    endorse   statement   interest

A _____ 's check is a bank's own check.

    cashier   pending   service

When you move, notify the bank of your change of address.

Words and Meanings

Say the banking word out loud and read its meaning. Read the sentence that follows. Then find and circle the banking word in the sentence.

Deposit (di PAHZ uht): *put in; money put into an account.*
I'll deposit $50 to my checking account.

Penalty (PEN uhl tee): *a fine.*
You pay a penalty for a late loan payment.

Regular (REG yuh ler): *a certain kind of.*
Most people have regular savings accounts.

Notify (NOHT uh figh): *tell.*
When you move, notify the bank of your change of address.

Outstanding (owt STAN ding): *not paid.*
When will you pay your outstanding loan?

Same Words

Check the word in each row that is the same as the first word in the row. Go as fast as you can. Time yourself.

Regular	Record	Register	Regular
Deposit	Deduct	Deposit	Depot
Outstanding	Statement	Outstanding	Outside
Notify	Apply	Notice	Notify
Penalty	Penalty	Payment	Percent

No. Correct _____

Time _____

27

Letter Squares

The letters in each square spell a word from the list at the top of page 27. Write the word or phrase below the square.

```
T N U
N O I S G
T D A
```

_____

Missing Vowels

To finish these words, fill in the missing vowels. Write the complete words on the blank lines.

pnlty _____

tstndng _____

dpst _____

rglr _____

ntfy _____

```
U A E
  R
R L G
```

_____

Pick a Word

Underline the word that belongs in the space. Then write the word in the space.

She made a _____ to her account.
    forward   deposit   service

Most people have _____ savings accounts.
    regular   service   savings

He had to pay a _____ for being late.
    statement   presence   penalty

Will the bank _____ me about my penalty?
    notify   apply   endorse

She paid off her _____ loan.
    balance   pending   outstanding

```
Y I F
  O
  T N
```

_____

```
O I E
  T
D S P
```

_____

```
A T E
  Y
P L N
```

_____

Review

The 15 words from the list on page 22 fit in this puzzle. The first and last letters of each word are given. The letters where the words cross are also given. Fill in the missing letters. Don't look back unless you have to. One word is done for you.

Test

Put a + by the sentence that is true. Put a ○ by the sentence that is not true.

_____ 1. Banks pay interest on savings accounts.

_____ 2. *Deposit* means to take money out.

_____ 3. Banks notify you if your loan is outstanding.

_____ 4. A father can be his child's trustee.

_____ 5. *Beginning* means regular.

_____ 6. You should endorse your paycheck in the presence of the teller.

_____ 7. *Penalty* means the same as *interest*.

_____ 8. Banks issue cashier's checks.

_____ 9. Traveler's checks are for people who go on trips.

_____ 10. Banks charge for certain services.

Unit Four

Safe Deposit Box   Banks rent safe deposit boxes to people who want to keep things in a safe place. People put the things in the boxes. Then the bank locks the boxes in a vault. What kinds of things might people keep in a safe deposit box?

_____

_____

Pretest

- ☐ capital
- ☐ average
- ☐ condition
- ☐ reverse
- ☐ investment
- ☐ minimum
- ☐ qualify
- ☐ renewal
- ☐ withdrawal
- ☐ credited
- ☐ overdraft
- ☐ currency
- ☐ adjustment
- ☐ applicant
- ☐ automatic

Buying this boat was a good investment.

Words and Meanings

Say the banking word out loud and read its meaning. Read the sentence that follows. Then find and circle the banking word in the sentence.

Capital (KAP uht uhl): *money.*

Your capital earns interest in a bank.

Average (AV uh rij): *between the highest and lowest.*

The average balance of this account is $100.

Condition (kuhn DISH uhn): *way something must be.*

The condition for this loan is: pay me back on Friday.

Reverse (ri VERS): *other; opposite.*

Forward your total to the reverse side.

Investment (in VEST muhnt): *money used to make money.*

Buying this boat was a good investment.

Same Words

Check the word in each row that is the same as the first word in the row. Go as fast as you can. Time yourself.

Condition	Conduction	Condition	Conclusion
Average	Average	Averse	Overage
Reverse	Regular	Reverse	Register
Capital	Capitol	Capital	Capture
Investment	Interest	Invite	Investment

No. Correct _____

Time _____

Word Wheel

Begin at Start. Find the first word. Put a line between it and the next word. One word follows another. Write the words on the lines as you find them.

_____

_____

_____

_____

_____

Start ▶ CAPITALCONDITIONINVESTMENTAVERAGEREVERSE

Missing Ink

Complete the words by adding a curve or a straight line to each letter. Then write the words on the blank lines.

AVERAGE _____

REVERSE _____

INVESTMENT _____

CAPITAL _____

CONDITION _____

Pick a Word

Underline the word that belongs in the space. Then write the complete word in the space.

He put his _____ into a savings account.

    statement   slip   capital

A savings account is an _____.

    investment   trustee   penalty

The _____ for the loan is that you pay it back.

    occupation   condition   presence

Did you fill in the _____ side?

    reverse   presence   pending

What is my _____ balance for the year?

    funds   submit   average

I hope we qualify for a home improvement loan.

Words and Meanings

Say the banking word out loud and read its meaning. Read the sentence that follows. Then find and circle the banking word in the sentence.

Minimum (MIN uh muhm): *least; smallest.*

Is there a minimum deposit on this plan?

Qualify (KWAL uh figh): *to be fit for something.*

I hope we qualify for a home improvement loan.

Renewal (ri NOO uhl): *something started again.*

I'd like a renewal of my loan.

Withdrawal (with DRAW uhl): *money that is taken out.*

She made a withdrawal from her savings.

Credited (KRED uht uhd): *added to an account.*

Your deposit will be credited to your account.

Same Words

Check the word in each row that is the same as the first word in the row. Go as fast as you can. Time yourself.

Credited	Credible	Checking	Credited
Minimum	Maximum	Minimum	Minimize
Qualify	Quantity	Quality	Qualify
Withdrawal	Withdrawal	Window	Withstand
Renewal	Personal	Record	Renewal

No. Correct _____

Time _____

Missing Vowels

To finish these words, fill in the missing vowels. Write the complete words on the blank lines.

rnwl _____

crdtd _____

wthdrwl _____

mnmm _____

qlfy _____

Scrambled Letters

The letters in each of the words are mixed up. Write the letters so they spell words from the list at the top of page 33.

mmniimu _____

qafuyil _____

thirdlawwa _____

dicetred _____

warlene _____

Pick a Word

Underline the word that belongs in the space. Then write the word in the space.

She made a _____ from the bank.
    penalty   withdrawal   trustee

A good payment record helps you _____
for a loan.
    vault   total   qualify

His deposit was _____ to his account.
    credited   optional   average

You must put in a _____ deposit.
    endorse   capital   minimum

They received a _____ of their loan.
    forward   renewal   checkbook

Are you an applicant for a loan?

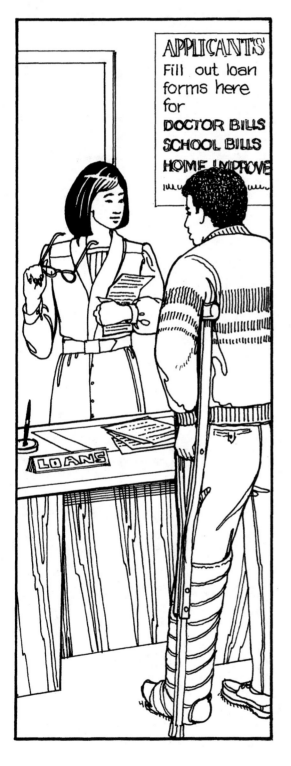

Words and Meanings

Say the banking word out loud and read its meaning. Read the sentence that follows. Then find and circle the banking word in the sentence.

Overdraft (OH ver draft): *a check for more money than an account has.*

Most banks give a penalty if you make an overdraft.

Currency (KER uhn see): *paper money.*

She listed her currency and checks on the deposit slip.

Adjustment (uh JUHST muhnt): *a change or correction.*

The teller made an adjustment in my passbook.

Applicant (AP li kuhnt): *person who asks for something.*

Are you an applicant for a loan?

Automatic (awt uh MAT ik): *done without asking; done by machine.*

The bank makes an automatic deposit to my account every month.

Same Words

Check the word in each row that is the same as the first word in the row. Go as fast as you can. Time yourself.

Adjustment	Investment	Applicant	Adjustment
Automatic	Average	Automatic	Autograph
Overdraft	Overcast	Overdraw	Overdraft
Applicant	Adjustment	Applicant	Appetite
Currency	Currency	Curtain	Current

No. Correct _____

Time _____

Letter Squares

The letters in each square spell a word from the list at the top of page 35. Write the word below the square.

Missing Ink

Complete the words by adding a curve or a straight line to each letter. Then write the words on the blank lines.

APPLICANT _____

OVERDRAFT _____

CURRENCY _____

ADJUSTMENT _____

AUTOMATIC _____

Pick a Word

Underline the word that belongs in the space. Then write the word in the space.

Banks can make _____ deposits for you.

   automatic   charge   pending

He is the _____ for this loan.

   transfer   balance   applicant

The bank made an _____ for its mistake.

   opening   adjustment   investment

Add up your _____ , coins, and checks.

   condition   currency   reverse

He received a penalty for his _____ .

   interest   occupation   overdraft

P I P
C T N
A A L

_____

M E D
S N U J
A T T

_____

U R N
Y C
C E R

_____

T T M
C A O
U A I

_____

A D R E
O R
F V T

_____

Unit Four

Review

The 15 words from the list on page 30 fit into this puzzle. They go across and down. The sentences and number of spaces will help you. As you find the words, write them in the spaces in the sentences. One is done for you.

Across

1. Banks give a penalty if you make an _____overdraft_____ .

4. _____ is money.

5. A _____ is money taken out.

6. An _____ asks for something.

9. Money used to make more money is an _____ .

11. _____ means the smallest.

13. Dollar bills are _____ .

14. _____ is not the highest or lowest.

Down

2. _____ means by itself.

3. You may borrow on the _____ you pay back.

6. An _____ fixes mistakes.

7. A _____ starts something again.

8. Your deposits are _____ to your account.

10. You must _____ to get a loan.

12. _____ means other side.

Crossword grid: 1 across OVERDRAFT

Test

Answer the questions below. Write *yes* or *no* in front of each of them.

_____ 1. Is an overdraft an investment?

_____ 2. Do banks ask for minimum deposits?

_____ 3. Does *renewal* mean withdrawal?

_____ 4. Does *currency* mean dollar bills?

_____ 5. Do banks make adjustments?

_____ 6. Can an applicant ask for a loan?

_____ 7. Does *reverse* mean the same side?

_____ 8. Do banks give loans on the condition you pay back?

_____ 9. Does *average* mean the highest?

_____ 10. Does *automatic* mean to qualify?

Unit Five

Automatic Teller Machine Some banks have automatic teller machines. These machines are found outside the bank or in shopping malls. They can be used any time, day or night, to deposit money or get cash. Why are automatic teller machines useful?

_____

_____

Pretest

- ☐ unlimited
- ☐ transaction
- ☐ delinquent
- ☐ certified
- ☐ compounded

- ☐ bank card
- ☐ ATM
- ☐ PIN
- ☐ financial
- ☐ guarantee

- ☐ authorize
- ☐ separately
- ☐ references
- ☐ responsible
- ☐ maturity

- ☐ personalized
- ☐ certificate
- ☐ signature card
- ☐ individual
- ☐ insufficient

He collects delinquent payments.

Words and Meanings

Say the banking word out loud and read its meaning. Read the sentence that follows. Then find and circle the banking word in the sentence.

Unlimited (uhn LIM uht uhd): *as many as you want.*
You may make unlimited withdrawals.

Transaction (tranz AK shuhn): *a business deal.*
Getting a bank loan is a transaction.

Delinquent (di LIN kwent): *late.*
He collects delinquent payments.

Certified (SERT uh fighd): *backed by the bank's promise to pay.*
I got a certified check from my bank to pay for my new car.

Compounded (kahm POWND uhd): *paid at certain times.*
Interest is compounded daily on this account.

Same Words

Check the word in each row that is the same as the first word in the row. Go as fast as you can. Time yourself.

Certified	Certified	Credited	Certain
Delinquent	Deductions	Delinquent	Delay
Unlimited	Unlisted	Unlimited	Unlined
Compounded	Condition	Compounded	Combined
Transaction	Transaction	Transfer	Transmit

No. Correct _____

Time _____

Word Wheel

Begin at Start. Find the first word. Put a line between it and the next word. One word follows another. Write the words on the lines as you find them.

_____

_____

_____

_____

_____

Scrambled Letters

The letters in each of the words are mixed up. Write the letters so they spell words from the list at the top of page 39.

tedqlunine _____

dulnitmie _____

docnopumed _____

friedtice _____

snacratnoit _____

Pick a Word

Underline the word that belongs in the space. Then write the word in the space.

There is a penalty for _____ payments.
   financial   delinquent   capital

Buying a car is a _____ .
   presence   renewal   transaction

_____ checks are backed by a bank.
   Certified   Cash   Currency

Interest is _____ daily on this account.
   penalty   compounded   deducted

You can make _____ withdrawals.
   funds   capital   unlimited

You must enter your PIN when you use an ATM.

NEVER TELL ANYONE YOUR PIN

ENTER YOUR PIN XXXX

Words and Meanings

Say the banking word out loud and read its meaning. Read the sentence that follows. Then find and circle the banking word in the sentence.

Bank Card (BAYNK KAHRD): *a card that has your name and account number on it.*

You need a bank card to cash a check here.

ATM (AY TEE EM): *Automatic Teller Machine.*

You need a bank card to use an ATM.

PIN (PIHN): *Personal Identification Number; a private code that signals who you are.*

You must enter your PIN when you use an ATM.

Guarantee (gar uhn TEE): *promise to make good.*

Banks guarantee their certified checks.

Financial (fin AN chuhl): *having to do with money.*

Banks offer loans and other financial services.

Same Words

Check the word in each row that is the same as the first word in the row. Go as fast as you can. Time yourself.

ATM	AIM	ATM	MAT
Bank Card	Bank Card	Bank Loan	Banks
Financial	Finance	Financial	Forward
Guarantee	Guarantee	Garnish	Currency
PIN	PAN	PIN	PUN

No. Correct _____

Time _____

Letter Squares

The letters in each square spell a word from the list at the top of page 41. Write the word below the square.

Missing Vowels

To finish these words, fill in the missing vowels. Write the complete words on the blank lines.

grnt _____

TM _____

PN _____

bnk crd _____

fnncl _____

Pick a Word

Underline the word that belongs in the space. Then write the word in the space.

An _____ is often in a shopping mall.

    ATM   AIDS   PIN

To use an ATM, you need a _____.

    loan   bank card   reference

A _____ statement lists your expenses.

    faster   financial   final

A _____ is a kind of promise.

    loan   due   guarantee

Never tell your _____ to anyone.

    ATM   ZIP   PIN

AN
BCA
KRD

_____

M
A
T

_____

C L A I
N F
I N A

_____

R A E
T N A
G U E

_____

N
I
P

_____

You must learn to be responsible for your bank account.

Words and Meanings

Say the banking word out loud and read its meaning. Read the sentence that follows. Then find and circle the banking word in the sentence.

Authorize (AW thuh righz): *give the right to do; OK.*

You authorize a withdrawal when you sign this slip.

Separately (SEP ruht lee): *one at a time.*

List your checks separately on this slip.

References (REF ruhn suhz): *people who can tell good things about you.*

You need references to get a bank loan.

Responsible (ri SPAHN suh buhl): *can be blamed; must answer for.*

You must learn to be responsible for your bank account.

Maturity (muh TOOR uh tee): *end of a period of time.*

This loan must be paid in full by its maturity date.

Same Words

Check the word in each row that is the same as the first word in the row. Go as fast as you can. Time yourself.

Separately	Safety	Separate	Separately
Responsible	Renewal	Responsible	Respond
Maturity	Maturity	Monthly	Maturing
Authorize	Author	Authorize	Authority
References	References	Register	Referents

No. Correct _____

Time _____

Word Wheel

Begin at Start. Find the first word. Put a line between it and the next word. One word follows another. Write the words on the lines as you find them.

_____

_____

_____

_____

_____

Start ▶ AUTHORIZERESPONSIBLESEPARATELYREFERENCESMATURITY

Missing Ink

Complete the words by adding a curve or a straight line to each letter. Then write the words on the blank lines.

REFERENCES _____

AUTHORIZE _____

SEPARATELY _____

RESPONSIBLE _____

MATURITY _____

Pick a Word

Underline the word that belongs in the space. Then write the word in the space.

The bank is _____ for keeping my money safe.

    compounded   average   responsible

Checks should be listed _____ .

    separately   optional   registered

You may _____ the bank to make automatic loan payments.

    delinquent   authorize   applicant

Some savings plans have a _____ date.

    apply   occupation   maturity

The bank will ask you for _____ .

    references   apply   maturity

All my things are personalized.

Words and Meanings

Say the banking word out loud and read its meaning. Read the sentence that follows. Then find and circle the banking word in the sentence.

Personalized (PERS nuh lighzd): *marked with your name.*

All my things are personalized.

Certificate (ser TIF i kuht): *paper showing you own or have a right to something.*

A savings bond is a certificate.

Signature Card (SIG nuh cher KAHRD): *bank card that shows a person's written name.*

The teller checked a signature card before he cashed my check.

Individual (in duh VIJ wuhl): *one; separate.*

They each had an individual account.

Insufficient (in suh FISH uhnt): *not enough.*

She had insufficient funds in her checking account.

Same Words

Check the word in each row that is the same as the first word in the row. Go as fast as you can. Time yourself.

Insufficient	Insufficient	Individual
Signature Card	Signature Card	Safe Deposit
Personalized	Penalized	Personalized
Certificate	Certificate	Certified
Individual	Interest	Individual

No. Correct _____

Time _____

45

Missing Vowels

To finish these words, fill in the missing vowels. Write the complete words on the blank lines.

crtfct _____

sgntr crd _____

prsnlzd _____

nsffcnt _____

ndvdl _____

Scrambled Letters

The letters in each of the words are mixed up. Write the letters so they spell words from the list at the top of page 45.

lansporedezi _____

icetinfinfus _____

rageituns drac _____

lividdinua _____

faceittrice _____

Pick a Word

Underline the word that belongs in the space. Then write the word in the space.

His wife has an _____ account.

    penalty   individual   less cash

This _____ has a maturity date.

    certificate   references   statements

Never write a check on _____ funds.

    enough   capital   insufficient

The bank keeps a _____ on file.

    signature card   minimum   less cash

Her name and address are on her _____ checks.

    currency   personalized   safety

Review

The 20 words below are hidden in the puzzle. They are printed in a straight line. But they may read across, up, down, backwards, or on a slant. Some words overlap. Circle the words as you find them. Then cross them off the list.

~~ATM~~ AUTHORIZE
TRANSACTION SEPARATELY
DELINQUENT REFERENCES
CERTIFIED RESPONSIBLE
COMPOUNDED MATURITY
BANK CARD PERSONALIZED
UNLIMITED CERTIFICATE
FINANCIAL SIGNATURE CARD
GUARANTEE INDIVIDUAL
PIN INSUFFICIENT

```
S E L B I S N O P S E R C A R A L
W I N D I V I D U A L C E T S D P
M G G T O Q X N R D L R R P E D E
T R A N S A C T I O N C T L P I R
C B R S A U A P G B H I I E A T S
C J N B A T M O N A L N F D R I O
O M O A L H U Q R T Q E I C A O N
M C K N F O V R W U X B C H T N A
P D G K I R Y Z E A S B A C E A L
O F M C N I N N K C J L T E L L I
U N P A A Z T O Q T A U E V Y W Z
N S T R N E Y X G U A R A N T E E
D Z A D C E R T I F I E D R V O D
E C E P I N N F N P Q S T U W X J
D D I N A A L M M A T U R I T Y N
B J U N L I M I T E D X K J I M C
Y Z A E D I N S U F F I C I E N T
R E F E R E N C E S L B H L E A H
```

Test

Answer these questions. Write *yes* or *no* in front of each question.

_____ 1. Everyone has the same PIN.

_____ 2. Financial has to do with paper.

_____ 3. *Automatic* means delinquent.

_____ 4. A bank card looks like a charge card.

_____ 5. A signature card shows a written name.

_____ 6. Personalized checks are references.

_____ 7. *Separately* means one at a time.

_____ 8. *Unlimited* means certified.

_____ 9. Interest is compounded daily on some savings accounts.

_____ 10. Banks are responsible for keeping money safe.

_____ 11. An applicant asks for something.

_____ 12. ATM means automatic teller machine.

_____ 13. An overdraft is a guarantee.

_____ 14. Savings certificates have maturity dates.

Guide to Phonetic Respellings*

Many of the words in this book are followed by respellings. The respellings show you how to say the words.

A respelling tells you three things about a word:

1. How many sounds, or syllables, the word has
2. Which syllable to stress
3. How to say each syllable

Look at the chart below. It shows you how to say each part of a respelling.

Now look at the word below. Then look at the respelling that follows it.

example (ig ZAM puhl)

1. How many syllables does *example* have? (3)
2. Which syllable should you stress? (ZAM)
3. How do you say each syllable? (ig) (ZAM) (puhl)

Say **example** (ig ZAM puhl) out loud. Then practice saying these respellings:

practice (PRAK tuhs)   **syllable** (SIL uh buhl)
follow (FAHL oh)   **phonetic** (fuh NET ik)

If you see:	Say it like the:	In:		If you see:	Say it like the:	In:
(a)	a	pat		(m)	m	me
(ah)	a	father		(n)	n	no
(air)	air	fair		(ng)	ng	sing
(aw)	aw	paw		(oh)	oa	coat
(ay)	ay	day		(oi)	oy	boy
(b)	b	bee		(oo)	oo	too
(ch)	ch	chair		(or)	or	for
(d)	d	do		(ow)	ow	how
(e)	e	send		(p)	p	pay
(ee)	ee	see		(r)	r	row
(ehr)	err	merry		(s)	s	say
(er)	er	fern		(sh)	sh	she
(ear)	ear	hear		(t)	t	too
(f)	f	far		(th)	th	thin
(g)	g	go		(*th*)	th	the
(h)	h	he		(u)	u	put
(hw)	wh	where		(uh)	u	but
(i)	i	is		(v)	v	very
(igh)	igh	high		(w)	w	way
(j)	j	joy		(y)	y	you
(k)	k	key		(z)	z	zoo
(l)	l	lay		(zh)	s	treasure

*All respellings are based on pronunciations found in *Webster's New Collegiate Dictionary*, 8th ed. (Springfield, Mass.: G. & C. Merriam Co., 1974). Pronunciations may differ in your community or your geographic region.